REpossibility

The stories of companies that succeeded **because** of their challenges (not despite them)

by
WAYNE CERULLO

CONTENTS

1. The Power of REpossibility   5

2. From Goliath to Lazarus: 11
   The XEROX story

3. Increase 'Customer Focus'   25
   by Hiring One:
   The IBM story

4. Diamond (Buried) in the Rough: 37
   The DeBEERS story

5. How an Industry Laggard Flew   49
   Past its Competitors
   The CONTINENTAL AIRLINES story

6. The Innovation Waiting   61
   Right Next Door
   Birth of the Missouri Cone Company

7. Creating your own REpossibility   69

The Power of
REpossibility

It is natural that we all seek success in life. We all want to succeed. This is especially true in business, and even more in our competitive, success-driven culture. Which is what makes our topic of failure particularly taboo and particularly surprising.

The Great Recession of recent years forced us to think about the unthinkable. Even successful companies had to face the possibility of failure. And several unbelievably successful companies turned out to be just that.

We were in a moment of really having to question, well, everything. And that's not just past history. Any follower of the world economy knows that at any moment – this moment – we are all just a hiccup away from chain reaction of cascading events that turn our planetary system upside down.

These companies "succeeded not despite the challenges they faced, but because of them."

So one would think that the global Fortune 100 — the behemoths that rule the economy on planet earth — would be the few companies that had managed to steer their way through trying economic times without tripping.

But in the stories you are about to read about several of those leading companies a very different narrative is revealed. It is a narrative of failure, and not just a single, small mistake. Each faced a string of massive existential challenges that threatened the very life of the company. And somehow they escaped to become the world leaders we know them to be today.

What we found - and what surprised us - was that these companies were not lucky enough to skirt the jaws of defeat, but that they had marched right through this hellish crucible and emerged from the forge stronger, sharper, and more passionate about their future than when they went in! In a phrase, **they succeeded not despite the challenges they faced, but because of them.**

There is a great diversity in the settings of these stories -- from photocopiers to diamonds to ice cream – but there are two themes that connect them all. One is the searing need to understand and serve their customers better than ever before – and better than their competitors. The second theme is their complete unflinching dedication to do everything to act on that revelation.

- **Xerox** was saved from billions in debt and a looming chapter 11 filing by not just talking to their customers but truly listening and then growing to actually meet their needs.

- **IBM** pulled out of 70% stock price plunge by breaking outside its walls and hiring an outsider - a customer - who had such a freshly baked perspective that he was nicknamed the "Cookie Man" (there were more reasons).

- **DeBeers** caught a glimpse of what made their prospects tick in the middle of the Depression, redefined the meaning of their commodity to fit the times, and thus created a brand as strong as their product.

- **Continental Airlines** steered themselves away from a third Chapter 11 filing and ten straight years of losses by finding out what the customer actually cared about and then committing themselves to delivering it!

- And on a much smaller scale, immigrant Arnold Fornachou turned an operational disaster into something so completely novel that you'll just have to read what he invented.

INNOVATION IS A MOMENT, NOT A MONUMENT

Undoubtedly you have noticed that all of the companies cited in this book is shining examples of REpossibility have also faltered at another time in their history.

- IBM's sales and valuation have been lethargic for many years.

- Xerox failed in its bid to merge with Fuji and its bonds are rated as "junk".

- Continental was forced to merge with United to survive the cut-throat airline wars.

- DeBeers' was associated with "blood diamonds" and price fixing and saw its market share drop from 90% to 33%

You might initially think that this taints the validity or importance of the stories recounted in this book. But that would be a misinterpretation.

The truth is that the need to put an innovative focus on meeting your customers' needs is not an act that is "one and done". Customer focus is a continuing requirement for success as your customer base and dynamic competitive frame continue to evolve. When companies lose this focus (again), they pay for it. Their later misfortune only reinforces the need to stay vigilant.

The purpose of these stories, of course, is not just to entertain. It is to inspire. First, they demonstrate with verifiable historical certainty that even if your company is on the brink of extinction, it can still not only survive, but thrive. The keys are simple but not easy. You will notice that all were pushed to focus relentlessly on understanding and delivering on what their customers needed better than anyone else. And for that, their customer base responded by resurrecting them to serve another day.

But there is a broader application, one for companies not about to go under. Hopefully that applies to you. Hopefully you are able to look at these real-life examples and apply their lessons before you are brought so low. Certainly we can fare better if we apply these lessons when we still have some health. As Paul Romer observed, a crisis is a terrible thing to waste. Our hope is that we all can take courage to focus our companies

Paul Romer
Chief Economist, World Bank

on why we are here no matter where we are starting from. Let's start now.

From Goliath to Lazarus

Xerox is revived by the power of customer led innovation

This case study examines the lessons from one such "Number One", Xerox, which realized that its size and market position were actually acting as a hindrance to growth. Specifically, it offers the reader useful lessons in:

- *How success can breed complacency and lay the ground for a fall*

- *How to bring together employees to re-build a company and*

- *How to truly be customer-driven and innovative*

Staking out a claim in the market as an industry leader is tough, but holding onto that position can be even more difficult. The story of Xerox is one of how the number one global document-management company (and a name synonymous with the photocopying business) rapidly lost its hold on the market and accrued several hundred million dollars in debt.

Xerox's enormous success led to complacency that in turn allowed management to think that they could get away with ignoring customer-centric innovation. Competition soon had a product edge, costing Xerox its position as the industry leader and leading to near-bankruptcy. CEO Anne Mulcahy, however, seized on the crisis to implement radical changes – including a re-commitment to opening lines of communication with customers and developing cutting-edge product lines and services that eventually turned around the company.

INSERT SUPERHERO METAPHOR HERE

The low rumble of the plane's engine was having a soporific effect on Mulcahy. She could feel her eyes growing heavier and her grip on the notes she had been going over loosen. She knew she should just give in and indulge in a few well-deserved moments of rest, but there was too much to be done. There was a lot of expectation to live up to as the company's first female CEO – especially as pundits were waiting in the wings, ready to pounce on the fact that she came from sales and HR, which didn't exactly fit the traditional profile of a corporate leader. Not too mention the pressures of reviving a company $17 billion in debt, facing an SEC scandal, and on the brink of filing for Chapter 11. No, sleep was not an option.

Mulcahy straightened up in her seat and reached for the complimentary coffee. There was no way she was going to give the naysayers the smug satisfaction of watching Xerox fail, which was precisely why she had spent nearly 90 days flying from meeting to meeting, speaking with CEOs, and industry analysts. It was also why she had arranged countless public forums and focus-groups for customers and was actively encouraging them to send in feedback. She wanted to know as much as she could before devising a strategic plan – from outsider perspectives on Xerox products and client service to financial solutions and crisis-response techniques. Anne Mulcahy was going to revive Xerox and make it, once again, a company known for cutting-edge innovation that provided the top-of-the-line products customers wanted.

MEMORIES OF THE GLORY DAYS

Xerox had been the undisputed leader in document duplication. After launching the first plain-paper photocopier in 1960, the Xerox 914 Copier – the company quickly made a name for itself. Xerox products were not just part of the office machinery – they had revolutionized office culture. The product was named the Fortune 500's **"product of the**

year" and the company was hailed as one of the **"most important technological innovators of the century"**.

Over the course of the next eight years the copier line earned the company over $1 billion **in profits!** By 1969, Xerox had grown to become one of the 100 largest corporations in the United States. During the 60s, it seemed as if you could never go wrong buying Xerox stock.

THE FALL OF GOLIATH

By the end of the next decade, however, Xerox had already begun to lose its hold on the market, largely due to shifting focus from what had earned the company its laurels in the first place – customer - oriented, creative innovation.

Through the 80s, the company shifted its attention from its core business, spending much time and effort on unrelated acquisitions in insurance and financial services. Despite the brilliance of its world-renowned PARC (Palo Alto Research Center), Xerox employed little of its work (although other companies famously did)!

Part of the problem was Xerox's success in photocopying. The field did not stay empty for long. Soon, **enterprising competitors** began to capitalize on the new document - duplication technology and launched their own – improved

– versions of Xerox's photocopier. Japanese companies such as Ricoh and Canon posed the stiffest competition with their less expensive, smaller, and more reliable models.

Xerox, meanwhile, was entering a period of developmental stagnation. There was **little focus on improving products** to keep the customers returning. Xerox had become virtually synonymous with photocopying, so the company believed they would continue to be leaders without doing anything particular to keep that title. In fact, by 1985, Xerox's plain-paper copier **market share collapsed** from 85% in 1974 to 40%.

INTO THE EYE OF THE STORM

Xerox continued to plod along for the next decade, although no longer the industry leader. In the late 1990s, however, the company faced a crisis that made it clear that the hazy glow of its golden past was in its final hours. In the last months of 1999, Xerox stock plummeted after the company was forced to announce that profits were going to fall far short of what industry analysts had predicted. Although several external factors precipitated the crash, it was internal issues that really ushered in the crisis.

Efforts to radically change the company culture had gone awry. Multiple restructuring changes led to countless botched sales and shipping orders, dissatisfied customers, and a disgruntled workforce.

ONE FOOT IN THE GRAVE

As a result, the company ended up accruing some $16 billion in debt. The following year, Xerox's stock fell to 60 percent from its level in 1999 and in October 2000 the company reported a third-quarter loss of $167 million. As if the bottom line troubles were not enough, that winter, the SEC began investigating Xerox's accounting practices for the period from 1997 to 2000, which further eroded public confidence in the company. It seemed certain that the company was headed right for **Chapter 11.**

Preoccupied with these issues, Xerox was blind to the new opportunities opening up in the market. At this time, **office printers** were threatening to take over some of the turf traditionally occupied by copiers. In 1999, when U.S. inkjet printer sales reached $5.2 billion, Hewlett-Packard controlled 50% of the market, while Xerox managed a paltry 2%.

OUT OF THE ASHES:
REBUILDING FROM THE GROUND-UP

That was the point at which Anne Mulcahy was called in. The board ousted the former CEO and brought in a company veteran who had risen through the ranks from sales to HR management to become COO in the course of her 24-year tenure. There was such widespread shock at the announcement that Xerox stock fell by 15%. Not an auspicious start.

Because of her unconventional background, Mulcahy brought a **fresh perspective and openness** to creative solutions. She recognized that the real problem was more deep-seated than the Brazilian economic crash and poorly implemented restructuring that were frequently cited as performance anchors.

Ironically, Xerox had a kind of internal **superiority complex** – an assumption that Xerox had cornered the market for a reason and that was enough to keep the ship afloat. While the company paid lip service to the customer demand for new products, in reality, older product lines were rarely upgraded significantly. She believed Xerox was in dire need of a hearty dose of humility and the willingness to give customers what they actually wanted rather than the outdated models the company felt were "good enough".

This was why the first thing Mulcahy did as the new CEO was hop on the plane and begin meeting as many people with an interest in Xerox as possible. She wanted **constructive criticism** – the kind that had been ignored too long by previous executives.

THE RESURRECTING POWER OF A GOOD CRISIS

After opening the lines of communication and returning from her 90 days of soliciting input and advice, Mulcahy began to implement strategies that reflected the feedback she had been given. Doing so meant making some radical changes. And as it was a time of crisis, she realized that it was the perfect

opportunity to do so. With the company facing bankruptcy, there would be more **willingness to try** solutions that in other, more stable, periods might have been vetoed or received with reluctance. Her intuition

was right. When taken into confidence, most Xerox employees agreed to do **whatever it took** to save the company, so long as they were given a clear direction.

"A CRISIS IS A TERRIBLE THING TO WASTE"
– PAUL ROMER, STANFORD UNIVERSITY

Part of this meant taking a **"back to basics"** approach that focused on operational and structural efficiency as well as cutting expenditures by 50%. This required knowing what areas of the company were no longer viable and had become resource drains. If interest hadn't been expressed in a product- line, it got cut. For instance, she oversaw elimination of nearly all product lines aimed at the small office/home office business segment. She also sold off the subsidiaries in

China and Hong Kong to Fuji Xerox for $550 million and then halved its ties to Fuji for another $1.3 billion. There were also significant reductions in other sales and administrative expenses.

FROM INTERNAL HUBRIS
TO CUSTOMER-CENTRIC INNOVATION

Most importantly, however, Mulcahy aggressively went after lost markets by focusing on development of new products. As she later said to the Stanford Graduate School of Business, "Even with all of the cost cutting we did, we didn't take a dollar out of research and development." However, this emphasis on innovation was based on the customer and employee feedback calling for improved digital and color copiers and enhanced multifunction devices capable of printing, copying, scanning, faxing, and e- mailing. Under her direction Xerox debuted 38 new products along with a wide range of new document- related services in 2002 and 2003 alone.

At the same time, the company realized that customers were not always technologically savvy enough to tell them what they wanted. The company therefore began involving customers in its R&D labs, to show them what was possible, and therefore make the development process itself customer focused. Senior managers were no longer preoccupied solely with the P&L or with internal issues. Instead, each senior manager was assigned as a "focused executive" for a **key customer.** Mulcahy believed that unless **top management walked the talk** when it came to customer experience, other employees would not follow.

Mulcahy's strategy of open communication and receptivity to improvement proved to be exactly what the doctor ordered. The company's new willingness to innovate based on actual input rather than being driven by assumptions led to soaring revenues. Although it took a few years to fully emerge from the hole, **Xerox went from annual losses of over $200 million to grossing over $1 billion in less than five years.** Forbes declared Mulcahy to be one of the top ten "Most Powerful Women in America" in 2005.

Today, Xerox continues to swear by its culture of customer experience led innovation. The company no longer defines itself by its products but considers itself a **"services led technology company"**. In 2009, **two-thirds of the company's revenues came from new products** introduced in the prior two years and the company continues to be bullish on investing in areas such as green technology that will make a significant difference to future consumers.

LESSONS FOR US

1. **Focus innovation on serving customers, not products.** Rather than working for your company, imagine that you have been hired by the customer to develop products that solve their problems... oh, sorry – that's actually what you're doing!

2. **Innovation and Improvement are essential:** As Mulcahy knew, even in times of crisis, continuing to develop cutting-edge products is key to maintaining an edge in the market. As Jeff Bezos says, "Every day is day one" in innovation.

3. **Don't just listen -- respond to feedback:** Communication with customers, employees and industry experts can provide critical insight into how to improve existing products or to move in new, more high-demand directions. In the age of empowered customers, paying lip service to input will backfire – especially in motivated, educated technology markets!

4. **No change can happen without employee consent:** It wasn't as if Xerox hadn't tried to change before. However, radical change worked only when employees truly saw the need for change and participated willingly in the process.

5. **Top Management must walk the talk:** Customer service and experience can easily become buzzwords that no one truly cares about. While compensation is important, employees are motivated to serve customers only when they see top management following the same principles.

A Fallen Empire of "impossibilities"	An Empire of "repossibilities"
▪ $200 million in debt ▪ Slipped from First to Low Position on the Industry Ladder ▪ Lack of innovation and sticking with "old and trusted" products ▪ Reluctance to be Open to Outside Input ▪ Relying on Laurels	▪ $1 Billion annual profit ▪ One of the Top Global Industry Leaders ▪ Focus on innovation and improving older products ▪ Receptivity to Outside/Customer Advice ▪ Constantly Demonstrating Why You're an Industry Leader

Increase 'Customer Focus' by Hiring One

The IBM story

In the early 90s, IBM was fast losing its position as the leader of the IT industry. The company's profits on mainframe computers, its core area, were falling. By 1993, the share price had slid from the stratosphere to a measly $12, a fall of over 70% in five years. Few people realized how precarious its position was.

Yet, by implementing a plan that focused on radically changing the company culture to be more nimble and customer-focused, IBM not only averted disaster, but returned to profitability and global leadership in a rapidly changing industry.

This case study examines the lessons from one corporate whale that emerged victorious from what seemed to be a certain road to business failure. Specifically, it offers the reader useful lessons in:

- How company culture can make a significant difference to innovation and growth

- How to bring about a much needed change in culture and employee mindset

- How to drive employees towards creating customer focused solutions

AND NOW FOR SOMETHING COMPLETELY DIFFERENT

Lou Gerstner looked out at the audience from the podium at the front of the large conference room. Seated before him were around 50 of IBM's most important employees – the executives in charge of on-the-ground operations for the company's headquarters around the world. While there were many impressive individuals in the room, what he saw was a sea of white shirts – making him stand out even more in his blue button-down.

Yes, there was definitely a kind of old-fashioned, uniform insularity about them all. And now that the polite applause was tapering off, they were even all sitting of action designed to completely transform the corporate culture must have come as quite a shock.

But that was exactly what IBM needed and he had just unapologetically said as much. In fact, since he was in the business of shaking up the whole system, he might just go ahead and eliminate the dress code . . .

HARD TIMES FOR HARDWARE

Gerstner did, in fact, get rid of the company dress code shortly after that first executive meeting in early 1993. A minor issue in the larger scheme of things, IBM's white-shirt-and-tie dress code nevertheless said something about how the company had become obsessed with doing things the way "things had always been done." Gerstner, on the other hand, was an outsider more interested in finding new ways that actually got things done. And given the crisis at hand when he arrived, it meant finding new ways to do just about everything.

When Gerstner took over, the company was in serious trouble. IBM had made its name as the leader in mainframe technology and hardware manufacturing, which had dominated the business world since the 1950s. For decades, the three letters IBM were the symbol of excellence in the US and around the world. A career at IBM was a highly-sought prize by the best and the brightest. A perennial leader in patents and Nobel Prize laureates, IBM was not just a company – it was a veritable institution and model citizen. Its products were even featured in movies and its competitors were simply known merely as "IBM clones."

Beginning in the 1980s, however, the market began to move away from the larger data processing machines like IBM's System 360 to smaller personal computers. As this happened, IBM's primary revenue source began to drop like a stone. In the first three years of the 1990s, hardware sales dropped 50% leading to a loss of over $14 million. Meanwhile, though the company had begun to explore production of smaller microprocessors, it was far from enough to offset the sinking profits. In 1991 the company had to report that it was $1 billion in the red. And by the following year, they announced a loss of $8.1 billion – at the time the largest annual loss in corporate history.

It became clear that IBM would have to cut tens of thousands of jobs for survival, and some industry analysts even thought

IBM was headed for bankruptcy. With the company in utter disarray, in 1993 John Aker stepped down as CEO, and Louis Gerstner left his position as CEO of Nabisco to bring the company back from the brink.

THE CEO WHO WAS A CUSTOMER FIRST

As an outsider who had cut his teeth at McKinsey before heading American Express and most recently served as the "**Cookie Man**," or CEO of Nabisco, Gerstner had a unique vantage point that proved to be the exact corrective needed to turn IBM around. After all, as he liked to say, he was a longstanding IBM customer himself. At American Express, he had seen the arrogance with which IBM treated its customers.

What Gerstner could see that those on the inside could not, was that it wasn't simply the company's inability to keep up with the external crisis of a changing market. After all, IBM had been at the vanguard of the PC revolution. Nor were mainframes finished – they were critical for every large company. The problems were far more deep-seated than that – **the real threat was coming from within.**

One of the issues was structural – IBM had effectively become a "parts" manufacturer. Under Aker, there had been a major organizational shift underway towards **horizontal integration** that led to outsourcing and **atomized departments** who operated independently and with little accountability. This resulted in a fatal lack of communication and coordinated efforts within the company. Even more problematic than the fragmented production line, however, was a bad habit of **departmental competition**. Rather than worrying about rival companies, the different divisions were more worried about outdoing each other.

The other real problem pertained to corporate culture – the company had grown **arrogant** and **inward-looking**. Or as Gerstner put it, IBM had become "inbred and ingrown." Despite the falling profits, the company continued to look at itself as the leader in cutting edge technology. For instance, all its software worked only with IBM hardware, although Microsoft, the acknowledged leader in the software space by then, had already changed the rules of the game.

Rather than being receptive to outside ideas, the various departments were effectively only drawing from within – borrowing ideas from competing divisions and rehashing old IBM concepts. It was like the company culture of white shirts and IBM-specific jargon – everything looked vaguely similar, was slightly out of date, and strictly geared for internal-use.

The confluence of this general attitude of insular arrogance with the tendency towards internal competition made for a deadly mix. **In the IBM world, the customer had been effectively eliminated from the equation.** And that, above all, was what Gerstner could see as an outsider.

From this perspective, he could see that there much work to be done on IBM's product lines and services before a customer would check-off the "highly satisfied" box. But, for this to happen, IBM needed to go from compartmentalized units to a cohesive, integrated whole that was working together towards a common goal -- satisfying the end-customer. In short, **IBM had to go from ego-centric to customer-centric.**

TAKING A HORSE TO WATER AND MAKING IT DRINK

The primary tasks at hand for Gerstner were to put a stop to the infighting and refocus attention on the customer. There was no way they could be competitive on the market if they were too busy shooting themselves in the foot all the time. This was of course easier said than done. It wasn't as if earlier management had never discussed the need for teamwork. He could take the horse to the water, but how was he to make it drink?

Part of the solution was fairly obvious; he needed to put the brakes on Aker's plan, which had already broken up much of the company into multifarious parts and was continuing to split the company into independent operating units. Gerstner realized that there would always be place for a top-tier consulting firm that could help customers get the best use from their technology purchases. IBM was best placed to do that, with its wide range of products and services. But, the company units had to stop thinking of themselves as selling individuals offerings and adopt a more holistic approach that leveraged all of the pieces of IBM – hardware, services and software – to deliver top-to-bottom technology solutions.

To incentivize the process, Gerstner implemented programs that rewarded teamwork over individual accomplishments. For instance, he mandated that every employee would make three "personal business commitments," or actions to fulfill broader IBM commitments. Performance against those commitments was directly tied to salary. He also created bonuses that were linked to the performance of the whole company rather than to the success of specific departments. Previously, there had been a lot of talk about 'the need to change', but these tough measures led employees to realize that their company was really going to be different, and that they had to change, if they wanted to reap the benefits.

To get employees' acceptance of the new plan, Gerstner began rolling out regular e-mails keeping them updated on the changes that he was bringing out. This kind of open communication with employees across divisions was itself something of a first for IBM. (Gerstner's book on the turnaround, 'Who says Elephant's can't dance?', talks about a European manager who actually blocked some of these mails because he thought they were 'inappropriate' for his staff!)

He also unified IBM's voice by consolidating its many advertising agencies down to one, Ogilvy & Mather. This reduced the competing confusion and mixed branding that IBM had profligately overwhelmed its customers with. Along with offering a unified service to customers, the company was going to offer one common brand message for all IBM products and services around the world.

Finally, it also meant making customer-driven financial decisions, like cutting products such as OS/2, the proprietary software system which had been a longstanding company favorite but a flop on the market. Large corporate software packages that were considered tried and true, but in actuality were cash-drains, also got the axe. The new IBM wasn't creating products for itself or out of respect for corporate custom; it was creating products for the customers. This in turn led to strategic choices about which divisions to downsize.

TURNING THE SUPERTANKER

Gerstner's plans revolutionized every aspect of IBM corporate culture – from dress codes to attitude and orientation. Blue and other color button-downs even became the norm as employees traded in their stodgy whites for a more relaxed look.

However, the new IBM wasn't just different in look and feel. It was also back in the black and once again a leader in the industry. By 1994, IBM was again solvent. IBM had achieved what was arguably the impossible, going from $8 billion in the hole to $3 billion in profit. And by the end of the decade, not only was IBM seeing year after year of increased growth, but was even being hailed as the **leader** of the newly emergent **'e-business'** market, a term that the company had coined.

Undoubtedly, much of this success derived from Gerstner's role as an outsider -- in fact the first outsider with to head IBM in eight decades. As he had no history with IBM, he was not afraid to make decisions that were radically different – and in some cases unpopular.  It also enabled him to approach the crisis without undue attachment to company canon. This gave him room to revamp management, lay off employees when necessary, and carve out new strategies. Most importantly, he **re-introduced the customer perspective,** moving IBM away from its inward looking attitude.

In so doing, he engineered **a complete turnaround for the company and led it from being a hardware manufacturer to a complete IT services corporation**. Cut to 15 years later - despite the economic slowdown and the pressure on IT spending, IBM is among the handful of companies that is able to predict a positive outlook for itself this year. Fifteen years since it was in the red, "Big Blue" is one of the tech industry's biggest success stories.

LESSONS FOR US

So why was IBM successful and what can we learn from it?

1. **Rejuvenation Begins with a Customer Perspective.** The enemy is not always on the outside. Companies that ignore customers for years can suddenly find themselves in a crisis, when the debt from years of neglect and mismanagement comes due. Companies need to remain customer-responsive.

2. **Continue to build.** Sitting on your laurels is a sure sign of decline, as Jim Collins identifies as one of the five stages of irrelevance in "How the Mighty Fall". Even the most exalted companies are subject to the same cycle of organizational entropy that besets "mortals."

3. **Even restructuring must have a customer bias.** Restructuring is not just about cost cutting or financial alignment. In the long term, restructuring brings positive results only when it is based on changing customer trends and industry movement.

4. **Enabling change needs objectivity.** Sometimes, company policy or thought is so entrenched that change becomes purely a buzzword. When change is not possible from inside, it must be driven from an objective outsider with no existing alliances or biases.

5. **Making change customer-relevant.** Change is not important for its own sake. Businesses must change because consumers change and competition changes. The only way to drive effective change is to do so from the perspective of the customer the company serves.

6. **Taking the team along.** Without employee commitment, change is impossible. Even during bad times, a fully-committed workforce can equip the company to do things otherwise not possible. However, employee commitment is not there for the asking. It must be built and nurtured.

From Navel-gazing Mainframe Maker	To Customer centric Information Leader
▪ Loss of $8.1 billion in 1991 ▪ Famous for internal division competition ▪ Product focused ▪ Proud and closed-minded ▪ Closed culture with little communication at lower levels ▪ Stodgy "white shirt" culture with uniformity being encouraged	▪ Positive outlook on revenues even during the current recession ▪ Cohesive company working towards common goals ▪ Customer oriented and working towards innovation ▪ Communication with all employees to get them on board and work together (2nd Life) ▪ Open to change, tele-commuting, more informal

Created

Diamond (Buried)
in the Rough

The DeBeers story

The Great Depression ravaged the economy for a decade and luxury items such as diamonds were particularly hard hit. Even DeBeers was on the brink of folding. By redefining their role in the value chain, and by changing the idea of what a diamond "meant", DeBeers not only managed to stay afloat, but laid the foundation for astonishing growth. Thus, a commodity mining company became a household name that forever changed the way the world expresses love.

This case study examines the lessons learned by a 'commodity marketer' who fundamentally changed the value that customers placed on its commodity offering and made it an essential part of customers' lives. Specifically, it offers the reader useful lessons in:

- *How end users and buyers have different motivations, and choosing whom to sell to is critical*
- *Why customers appreciate a brand even in a commodity market*
- *How emotional connect is critical to building brands, even at the worst of times*

IN SEARCH OF SALVATION

One day in September, 1938, Harry Oppenheimer, Jr. could already make out the distinct facade of the N.W. Ayer & Son building a short distance to the northwest, as he walked through the square. Though he was seeing it for the first time, there was no question that this was the right place. Home to the first advertising company in the United States, the ten year old building was already considered a fine example of Art Deco architecture.

Although only in passing, Oppenheimer thought to himself that it seemed like a somewhat ironic relic of the not-too-distant past as it had only been completed a year before the Crash of '29, when everything took a nosedive as the Depression set-in. He also couldn't help feeling a little hopeful; perhaps the awe he felt looking at the grand building as he approached it was an auspicious sign. He hadn't travelled all the way to Philadelphia from South Africa, however, to reflect on modern architecture. He had come to enlist the services of what was considered the most experienced advertising agency in America in order to save his family's jewels – the DeBeers diamond company.

HARD TIMES FOR HARD ROCKS

Like so many other luxury product firms, since the onset of the Depression, DeBeers had fallen on very hard times. Diamonds were simply not a viable commodity in such a climate. Demand was so low that the company had to reduce production from over 2 million carats before 1930 to only 14 thousand carats by 1933 – less than one percent of the prior volume! Despite having cut production to a trickle, there was a stockpile of unsold diamonds by 1937 – people simply weren't buying!

As a wholesaler, DeBeers primarily focused its attention on selling its products to large manufacturers, who then worked with the jewelers, who in turn worked with individual shops. The diamonds would eventually end up on the tennis bracelets of sporty young wives, or the cuff links of debonair entrepreneurs, but it was the companies in the supply chain who did the actually buying from DeBeers. And they simply weren't buying. Why would they? If business men weren't inclined to splurge on jewelry for themselves or their wives, what reason would there be to stock-up in bulk?

Earlier in the decade, his father had attempted to reinvigorate the market by shutting down their major mines to promote scarcity and cut back on costs. Since diamond prices in Europe had collapsed, he believed that an artificial scarcity would make them more valuable and get the company better prices. While the move cut costs, sales simply didn't pick up after this move. Many European countries such as Germany and Italy had no tradition of diamond rings being gifted at an engagement or any other event. In other countries such as the U.K, diamonds were seen as super-expensive objects meant for a small aristocracy. And now, with a major war brewing in Europe, luxury items like diamonds would be even less in demand. The company was in trouble – serious trouble. They were barely afloat as it was. Oppenheimer decided that he would need to place all his eggs in the American basket. Not just that, the new market would have to be dealt with very differently.

MAKE THEM BEG FOR MORE!

Despite the failure of his father's plan, Oppenheimer still felt that it had been a step in the right direction. It hadn't gone far enough, though. While the plan had focused on making the diamond rarer (and therefore something to be coveted), it hadn't done anything to stir demand among the people who would ultimately buy it. Oppenheimer felt absolutely certain that the end-customer was where they needed to focus their energies. If consumers wanted to buy diamonds, retailers would soon be begging DeBeers to give them more stock!

And that's precisely why he was now passing through those huge bronze doors as he entered 210 West Washington Square. Oppenheimer, Jr. was going to **remake DeBeers** from a mining company that sold wholesale gems to manufacturers, into a company that sold **diamonds to consumers.**

GETTING THE TRUTH
FROM THE HORSE'S MOUTH

Over the next several days Oppenheimer and a top team of N.W. Ayer's ad execs and copywriters began working on this task. As they sat at a desk in the firm's office overlooking the square they probed **the relationship between the end-customer and diamonds.** If they were going to talk to customers directly and get them to buy more, they needed to know what buttons to press. What, for instance, was so significant about diamonds? Why did people buy them? Who wore them and why? How did they make the recipient feel? In those days, consumer research wasn't common, but Oppenheimer felt these answers to these questions would give them the breakthrough they needed. He offered to pay for the cost of the research.

As the team worked together, they thought about the **current mood** around the world and where diamonds fit into that picture. With the dark clouds of the war brewing on the

American and Asian horizons, and Europe already under the heavy hand of totalitarianism and bloody conflict, people the world over were thinking of their loved ones, caressing their treasured keepsakes as they prayed for their safety and better days to come.

DeBeers research suggested that in over 90% of cases, it was young men who bought engagement rings. This implied that there was already a relationship between diamonds and romance. The retailer may be the one to buy the diamond from DeBeers directly, but it was that young wife who  saw her husband as she glanced at the delicate bracelet around her wrist. **A diamond wasn't a rare gem – it was a symbol of love and family.** Now they had to work on making that association even stronger. With war all around, DeBeers had to convey that diamonds were **more essential than ever.**

They set about this task by strongly associating diamonds with the courtship process. Movie stars were roped in to wear diamonds and fashion magazines talked about the diamonds that celebrities had been gifted as 'a symbol of love'. DeBeers also introduced subtle cues to highlight that the larger and finer the diamond, the better it reflected a man's love for his woman. This allowed the company to move the American market towards better quality (and higher priced) diamonds.

A (REPOSITIONED) DIAMOND IS FOREVER

Over the next several years, DeBeers began to regain its former success as people came to view diamonds as the

ultimate symbol of love. By 1941, the downward trend in retail sales had been entirely reversed, and in just three years, sales of diamonds in the United States rose 55%.

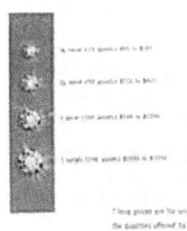

In the early 40s, the company acted to further strengthen the positioning it had adopted. Diamonds were now seen as a symbol of love, but to get even more people to buy one, they also had to convince them that diamonds were good value in themselves. It was a campaign in 1948, that did this and forever changed DeBeers and the diamond industry as a whole. It was in that year that Frances Gerety, a copywriter for N.W. Ayers, struggling to capture this new meaning, scrawled the message **"a diamond is forever"** on the bottom of a picture of two honeymooning lovers.

The company had already created a solid-foundation for themselves by establishing a relationship with the end-customer. Now, Gerety developed a slogan that suggested that diamonds were immortal. Not only could the wearer take pleasure in them, she could also pass it on to her children as a family heirloom and **an everlasting symbol of love.** It was simple, to the point, and a powerful message that appealed directly to the buyer – it was the ultimate tagline. Interestingly, the DeBeers name or logo did not feature in this campaign. The company reasoned that since it controlled the bulk of diamond mining, any growth in the market would automatically be to its advantage.

DIAMONDS FOR LASTING SUCCESS

With this campaign and other initiatives supporting the same message, Oppenheimer Jr. and N.W. Ayer's went on to successfully oversee one of the greatest company resurrections in business history. DeBeers not only **remade public understanding of the meaning of what a diamond represented,** but they also **spearheaded the birth of a new tradition – the diamond engagement ring.**

While diamond rings had been exchanged in the past, it was after Gerety penned her famous line that no bride-to-be was to be found without a sparkling diamond gleaming on her finger. It was also DeBeers who set the standard of two months salary on these rings. By 1960, the company found that many young people, who could not afford a diamond ring at the wedding, would still save up to buy one a little later. They repeated the American success in other countries around the world.

Today, sixty years later, the company continues to thrive and controls about 40% of the world diamond market. This is actually a come down from the days when DeBeers controlled 80% of the world diamond trade. In the 1990s, however, as many other companies entered the market, DeBeers continued to take its demand-led approach further and started focusing on quality diamonds from its own mines rather than surfeit quantity due to representing numerous others.

Since 2000, the company has launched "Forevermark", a global diamond brand promising quality and integrity (ethical mining and trading practices) in an attempt to gain a premium for its own diamonds. In 2008, DeBeers made gross profits of $1.2 billion, a slight increase over the previous year in difficult circumstances. Its long-term association with romance and love still makes it a preferred supplier for retailers and it enjoys better profitability than when it dominated trade and had to constantly work on creating scarcity. Today, DeBeers continues focusing on maintaining and strengthening the meaning of diamonds and translating it to newer, fast-growing markets such as India and China.

LESSONS FOR US

1. **Sometimes, demand is a latent fire that needs to be ignited.** Rather than remaining a passive purveyor of diamonds, DeBeers had the creativity to re-imagine its role in the market as a demand generator – not just fulfiller. Even amidst the direst of economic climates – including the Depression and the Second World War – DeBeers managed to stimulate demand by creating an emotional association between the product and customer that played directly off the international mood. DeBeers didn't fight prevailing trends, it reinterpreted them.

2. **A brand is a powerful tool – even for "commodities".** It's hard to imagine how radical it was for an African mining company to engage an American ad agency over a half-century ago. Brands can play an important role in any market.

3. **Be prepared to rethink** your customer set. By redirecting the marketing from its wholesale "near" customers to the consumer "next customer", DeBeers identified an audience that had never been directly addressed. Ultimately, what end customers wanted was what wholesalers and retailers wanted. DeBeers became successful – and distinctive – with its near customers by making them successful with their customers – a win/win!

4. **Turbulent, dramatic times call for dramatic measures.** The seismic shift of the last year and continued volatility are clear and permanent. But it's not the first time companies have had to deal with dramatic change. The combination of the Great Depression and World War Two for a luxury goods manufacturer

is more severe than what most companies are facing at this point. Yet DeBeers shows that it's not only possible to survive, but to thrive.

From Failing Wholesaler	To Customer centric Information Leader
▪ Virtually ceasing all diamond mining operations ▪ Marketing to Wholesale to ▪ Manufacturers and Major outlets ▪ Lack of Branding ▪ Foundering under the weight of a financial crisis ▪ Lack of Demand	▪ Controlling 40% of diamond operations ▪ Marketing to End-Customer ▪ Powerful slogan that used the climate to reinforce marketing ▪ Despite alternative diamond companies, culturally – speaking ▪ DeBeers remains virtually synonymous with diamonds in the public mind ▪ Created Demand by Creating a Market, that positioned diamonds as an iconic, symbol

How an Industry Laggard Flew Past its Competitors

The Continental Airlines story

In the early '90s Continental Airlines was considered one of the worst major commercial air carriers and nearing bankruptcy for the third time. At the crux of the crisis was universally low-morale within the company due to poor treatment of employees. For years Continental had pushed through ineffective cutbacks aimed at curbing costs at the expense of the workers. This led to a demotivated workforce with little incentive to be productive or to ensure customer satisfaction.

By implementing a plan that valued the workers and focused on creating a community committed to ensuring superior customer service, the company turned around within a year, rising to become one of the consistently top-rated and acclaimed airlines in the world.

This case study offers readers some interesting and practical lessons in:

- How to address the 'right problems' when it comes to customer satisfaction
- How to ensure that making the customer happy also keeps your bottom line healthy
- How to bring together employees to make things happen for the customer and for the business

BAD TROUBLE IN GOOD WEATHER

George Bethune stood staring out the window of his executive office overlooking downtown Houston. The sky was clear and bright - a perfect day for flying. He turned from the view and let out a sigh as he sank into his chair. No matter how beautiful the day was, it wasn't going to help Continental Airlines. After all, the weather wasn't the problem, it was everything else.

In early 1994, when the Board had called Bethune and asked him to take over as COO, he knew that the company was in trouble. That's precisely why they had contacted him; he had a great record at Boeing and before that, with other airlines. He knew what it took to salvage businesses on the brink of failure. He also knew what most travelers knew – when you fly Continental, forget any hope of arriving on time or receiving good service!

Even so, he had relished the opportunity to head the nation's fifth largest airline. Continental did not seem irredeemable to him – after all, many airlines were chronically behind schedule and as for issues caused by poor management, there would be few large organizations that hadn't faced such challenges. He figured that he would go in and do what needed to be done. So, by the time he was made CEO in November 1994, he received a few shocks discovering just how badly off the company really was.

TOP OF THE UNPOPULARITY CHARTS

During the previous decade, Continental had filed for bankruptcy not once, but twice, and was even on the verge of having to file for **Chapter 11 a third time**. Meanwhile, leadership had changed hands some ten times. In public polls and industry rankings, they were almost always voted among the worst. Out of the nation's top-ten largest airlines, Continental was the most likely to be over 15 minutes late. They were also responsible for damaging or losing more baggage than any other major airline. It was no surprise then that they received three times as many complaints as the industry average. In other words, **Continental was top of the charts when it came to the number of irate customers!**

Not surprisingly, the financial numbers reflected this. The stock had been steadily falling for years and the company had made no profits for years. In 1995, they had to report their **tenth straight year of losses.** It was the fifth largest airline but it was losing altitude fast! Bethune knew that time was running out. What he needed was a plan that amounted to a miracle -- a plan that had to tackle seemingly insurmountable problems head on.

With everything going wrong, there didn't seem to be a limit on the number of things that needed to be set right. And yet, everything pointed to one fundamental problem. **It was all about people.** Continental had long ago stopped respecting its employees and its customers. Employee morale was abysmally low, and understandably so. The previous CEO had made a habit of union-busting, resulting in a severely underpaid workforce, shockingly high work-related injuries, and nearly a 50% turnover rate.

Employees were outwardly ashamed to even admit that they worked for the company. It was common practice to take off the company pin when off duty just to avoid having other airport staff realize which airline they were affiliated with. These weren't the kind of staff who would care very much if a bag went missing or if customers were not greeted with a smile. No wonder customers suffered! In an effort to cut costs, frequent flyer programs had been slashed, making Continental even more unpopular with well-paying business travelers.

Bethune realized that if Continental wanted to crawl back from the dead-end it had reached, it had to start with putting customers first. And that was not going to happen magically. He decided that change had to begin with employees first. In a service industry, he could do nothing unless employees were motivated towards treating customers well and convincing them to fly Continental again. Deciding to begin with putting his own house in order first, he reached for the phone to tell his assistant to schedule a meeting with the Board. **It was time to reinvigorate his people with a purpose – that they were going to make people love to fly with Continental again.**

A FOUR-POINT PLAN TO WIN THEM BACK

As Bethune later wrote in his autobiographical account, by the end of 1995, Continental had gone from "worst to first." In less than a year, Bethune and his newly appointed wingman, COO Greg Brenneman, managed to engineer what is now considered one of the fastest and most formidable turnarounds in corporate history.

Continental

How did it all happen? Having realized that the problems were all with people, Bethune focused his solution on people as well. He launched the 'Go Forward Plan' – a program that above all focused on bringing satisfaction back to the people involved with Continental, whether as customers or employees.

Bethune and Brenneman identified four key areas, starting with providing the infrastructure for the company to succeed and ending with a focus on employee engagement in the cause.

The **first** fundamental step was **to offer services that people actually wanted.** This was the "Fly to Win" market strategy, designed to ensure that the airline was actually providing services that were in demand. This required re-routing to add popular destinations and in some cases ending service to less preferred areas. It meant changing ticket prices to better reflect comparable flights with other air carriers as well as customer expectations. Continental also brought back some of the frequent flyer programs that had been cut and started including food on some flights. This meant spending money, but it was **money spent carefully on services that mattered,** especially to business travelers who had previously been more than a little reluctant to fly a company known for shoddy service.

The **second** point – "Fund the Future" – focused on the financial end of the plan, again with an emphasis on ensuring customer satisfaction. As Bethune expressed it, "You can make a pizza so cheap that no one will eat it.  You can run an airline so cheap that no one will fly it." Instead of slashing costs, the new approach would be to spend more money **only in ways that would help to generate profit.** Reinvesting in the fleet, was one of the major ways to do so, including ordering new Boeing planes as well as making improvements to travelers' in-flight amenities and comforts.

While the new planes and changed routes were a start, the **third** goal to "Make Reliability a Reality" was perhaps the most directly related to improving customer service. Bethune declared to the force that he wanted their service to be like clockwork. From here on out, Continental was going to provide customers with a reliability they could always count on – from on-time departures to the general knowledge that they could always expect the highest-level of service from helpful and pleasant staff. To show that he meant business when it came to customer service, Bethune **linked company bonuses to on-time performance.**

Finally, the company needed to have a workforce willing to provide this to the customers, which is where "**Working Together**" came into play. In other words, he needed his team of 40,000 to want to actively work to meet these goals, which is why "Working Together" became the real rallying cry for the Go Forward Plan. This meant cultivating a community of satisfied employees who were actively invested in Continental's mission and wanted to see success for the company. At the time, Continental employees were still paid lower when compared to those with competing airlines. The plan therefore did include higher wages as well as some unique incentive programs. For instance, twice a year, a raffle was held for those with perfect attendance. The prize? Ford Explorers.

On the one hand, this approach did require allocating more of the budget for employee compensation. On the other, **the profit gained by doing this far exceeded the cost of not**

doing so. For instance, Brenneman calculated that it cost the company $5 million for every month that they were chronically late. One of the new incentives was to pay every employee $65 (approximately $2.5 million total) for any month the company ranked in the top-three for timeliness.

READY FOR TAKEOFF

Within months, Continental was already experiencing unprecedented, tangible results. In March 2005, Continental came in **first** for domestic on-time performance among the ten largest airlines. The next month they again ranked as number one. Then later that year, for four consecutive months – from August through November – they were named the best when it came to handling baggage. They also placed second in overall satisfaction and fewest complaints.

The sharply heightened level of service was not going unnoticed. Word was quickly spreading that **Continental was no longer synonymous for "poor service," but rather with "how to do it right."** And the numbers were proving it.

Employees were obviously more satisfied, and committed to the company (not to mention working under improved conditions) as evidenced by the decrease in turnover rate by 45%, worker compensation by 51%, and sick leave by 29%.

This was having a direct impact on overall sales as worker productivity sky-rocketed to meet the Go Forward challenge. And on July 18, 1995, **Continental announced the largest quarterly profit in its history.**

FROM WORST TO FIRST

By December 2005, things were even better. The stock price multiplied **fourteen times** from $3.25 per share to $47.50 and was named **Best NYSE Stock for the Year.** Moreover, the company ended the year having not only **made a profit for the first time in over a decade,** but the largest annual profit in the entirety of its 61-year history: $224 million! It was certainly a far cry from the $202 million loss of the previous year.

In 1996, they went on to see their **profit more than double** to $556 million. That year they also received the **J.D. Power Award for Best Airline** on flights of 500 miles or more. It was the first of countless awards to come. Since the initial implementation of the Go Forward Plan, Continental has remained committed to the principles set forth in it, each year identifying new ways to better live up to the four goals as needs and times have changed.

In so doing, even when faced with the external crises post-September 11th or the current financial collapse, they have remained at the top of all major national and global airlines in all categories – from Most Admired Global Airline to Best Executive Class Airline to Best Flight Attendants in the US.

LESSONS FOR US

1. **Inspire with purpose!** Change didn't start until the company had a big, provocative goal – one that benefitted customers and employees. Customers naturally seek value and the people in a company are created to fulfill a purpose. Extraordinary results come only from extraordinary efforts. Extraordinary efforts reflect relevant, credible goals and the sine qua non, trust. The resulting ROI on employee morale (14X in stock price alone) is, well, extraordinary!

2. **Employee commitment is not all about money.** While the money certainly communicates loudly, other elements like working conditions, management communication and recognition, make just as much impact on employee motivation.

3. **Spend Money to Make Money.** The increased cost of employee salaries and support programs certainly increased company costs. But it more than paid off in revenue, profits, and imagery. The goal, however, is to spend money in ways that most bolster customer and employee satisfaction. Increased profits come with increased investment.

4. **Manage costs, don't just cut them.** Hard times sometimes push management teams to cut costs wildly. But cost cutting by itself cannot grow revenues, which is the key problem. reduces expenis not an unqualified panacea for all problems. Cost management needs to take into account the potential loss of business or customers that may happen.

From Worst	To First!
▪ $3.25 per share ▪ $202 million in loss in a single year ▪ Rated Worst Customer Service ▪ Reputation as an Airline to Avoid ▪ Poor employee-employer relations; low productivity, high turnover rate, and higher resources spent on worker's comp	▪ 14X increase to $47.50 per share ▪ $556 million in profit in a single year ▪ Multiple Awards for Best Customer Service ▪ Reputation for Excellence ▪ Committed Team, ready to give 110% ▪ Less money spent on compensation and lost on late flights

The Innovation
Waiting Right
Next Door

Birth of the Missouri Cone Company

As the thermometer rose at one of the great World's Fairs during the summer of 1905, the fortunes of an ice cream vendor rose as well... until he ran out of glass dishes! Facing the potential loss of his he thought about dishes in a new way... and so invented a new industry and changed forever the way Americans eat dessert! But the real innovation came when he made the decision not to order more glass dishes!

THE FATAL FAILURE OF SUCCESS

There are two common fallacies about innovation. The first is about who does it and the second is about when it is done.

So far we have learned that companies that became the cornerstones of commerce — members of the global Fortune 500 — were once on the precipice of failure. But the power of REpossibility is that it can be kindled in any company... and even one-man startups!

The other fallacy is that innovation is what companies do when they have time and money to spare. We tend to think of innovation as the luxury of good times – what progressive companies do with the excess of current profits to sow future profits. They create "Chief Innovation Officers" and think tanks that brainstorm about the Next Big Idea.

AN AFTERNOON OF DESPERATION

You probably don't remember it, but the Louisiana Purchase Exposition of 1904 in St. Louis was celebrated in a terrific heat wave. And July 23 was particularly hot — which is why it is such an important date in innovation history.

It was especially terrific for one immigrant, Arnold Fornachou, who was fortunate enough to scrape together enough funds to purchase a vendor booth selling ice cream. He was thrilled to be selling at such a prestigious international event... and he wasn't disappointed! In fact, business was so brisk, he ran out of the glass dishes in which the ice cream was served! **Disaster!**

He had paid for the booth, made the ice cream, invested in refrigeration equipment, and attracted paying clientele!!! Only now he would have to send them away empty...unless he could come up with some other way to package the drippy substance so people could eat it without their soiling their petticoats... and fast!

In a panic, Arnold scanned around the other vendors in search of a solution, but no one served anything requiring a dish! Then he had an idea! Another immigrant vendor, Ernest Hamwi, was making flat, circular Syrian pastries called zalabia! (Hey, you can't make this stuff up!) Arnold folded the zalabia into a cone shape... and so the ice cream cone was born – not from new product development kitchens and focus groups, but from good old desperation! (Fortunately, there's still a lot of that around to spur problem-solving innovations today).

AND NOW FOR THE REAL INNOVATION

If Arnold had been thinking about merely maintaining business as usual after his World's Fair debacle, he would have instituted a six-sigma assessment to ensure that he had sufficient numbers of glass dishes and a rapid dishwashing process built into his market development plans. If Arnold had merely made it through a bad situation with a stopgap solution, we would not know any more about him.

The reason we celebrate Mr. Fornachou a century later is due to his being sufficiently open minded to recognize the long-term potential of his stopgap improvisation.

He went on to form the Missouri Cone Company (apparently he was not as good at naming inventions as he was at making them). By the time of the Depression, the 120 million men, women, and delighted children in America were consuming 250 million cones a year! He created not only a product, but a cultural transformation!

How often do you think the answer to our business problems might be right under our noses? It usually just takes someone to help us see them.

IS YOUR ICE CREAM MELTING?

What is the point of this story, as interesting as it is? (For ice cream fanatics, I understand no further explanation is needed)! I'll give a personal answer.

Aside from loving ice cream, this story is was the

inspiration for the development of this series of case studies. I was lamenting the apparent cessation of innovation when I chanced upon a program on the history of food in America.

When I heard this story about innovation that came only from desperation, I was encouraged to hear about the necessity and potential reward of innovation even – especially – in difficult times. It encouraged me to encourage companies to overcome impossibilities with "repossibilities".

FIVE WAYS TO WARM UP YOUR COMPANY PROSPECTS

Many companies have run out of "ice cream dishes" in today's distressed economic environment. Perhaps this depicts your company. This story reveals five keys to the success of your company:

1. **Difficult times, not just times of plenty, are great times for innovation.** In fact, history shows that the most dramatic, disruptive innovations come from the most difficult times and situations. Let us know if you want more examples.

2. **Innovations are closer than you think — it's a matter of seeing them.** Arnold was only a few stalls away from the salvation for his investment at the Louisiana Purchase Fair. But more than that, he was just a few stalls away from creating a completely new concept in an industry of which he didn't even view himself a part. It is possible to bring a fresh, outside-in perspective to your company that can unveil opportunities that you might be overlooking.

3. **You have no choice whether or not to innovate.** Your competitors are working on them as you read

this. If you're a culinary historian, you know there are multiple claims to the invention of ice cream. Rather than detracting from this account, it reinforces the urgency of acting quickly – because others, encountering challenges like yours, are also working on solutions while you contemplate.

4. **In times of disruptive volatility, competitors can come from anywhere.** Who would have thought that something as "American as ice cream" would come from the momentary collaboration of two unknown immigrant vendors at a fair! Similarly, you need to think beyond the competitors you know – the ones with your same training, assumptions, and business models. You need to think about potentially more disruptive competitors creating completely different solutions from completely different perspectives.

5. **The people in your company are poised for action.** Necessity is the mother of implementation. (We all know she also spawned innovation, but innovations never make it through childhood unless there is a powerful NEED to shepherd them through the often-toxic developmental environment of the corporation). The people in your company have never been more aware of the need for changing business as usual than now. This may be buried in the stress of fewer people having to do more work without a compelling vision for a way of changing the situation. The catalyst of an innovative response to the recession can be used to **engage them** in a way they have not yet been engaged.

If this story is relevant to your company, feel free to contact **B2P Partners** for a free consulting conversation about proven ways we can help your company see the overlooked opportunities within your grasp. We believe that every company is capable of accomplishing great things (or things that look great later) by taking a long view of the situation and striving for the greatest good. We don't try to tell you what you ought to be doing – we uncover and create it with you.

Let us know your interest in other historical case studies of companies that faced watershed moments at critical moments in facing major crises before they went on to become industry leaders such as IBM, Intel, Cisco, Motorola, Xerox, and Continental. We look forward to exploring new revenue streams with you.

Creating your own
REpossibility

I hope you have found the true stories in this mini - documentary of business histories to be illuminating, instructional, and even inspiring! I found them so encouraging that I decided they needed to be shared.

REACHING THE TOP
WITHOUT HITTING BOTTOM

Of course, each of these stories is dramatic. That's part of what makes them good stories. But it's not required that you bottom out before deciding to turn around.

Historical stories have always encouraged me with the idea that, if "they" could do that, then I can do this! Dramatic stories of desperate turnarounds instill us with confidence that our situation isn't nearly so bad as theirs, so certainly we can do what they did!

The message of this book – and indeed of companies that have turned their – is that revitalization is possible in nearly any situation.

These true tales of transformation point to a hidden truth – **your greatest weakness may be the launchpad for your greatest strengths.** A crisis is indeed a terrible thing to waste. And rather than being an anchor, your company's most troubling weaknesses may be your keys to success. Success is what should worry you!

Our mission:
Turn
impossibilities
into
repossibilities

But my hope is that we will wake up to the opportunity to turn around before we hit bottom!

HOW THEY GOT THERE

We introduced these cases with a bold claim that companies can actually become exceptionally successful by learning how to transform impossibilities into "repossibilities". But the opportunity to do this is not the same as actually doing it.

Fortunately, this is not magic. Looking at the turnarounds you read, you see there is a process to actually make this happen. There are five specific steps in these "marketplace restarts".

1. Candid Assessment of the External Environment

Each company turned their attention to outside their company walls to focus intently on the external challenges that were impinging on them. In some ways, each story is a tale of a company losing its focus on the external marketplace and how it was evolving.

The challenge is that, without a crisis to focus everyone on the importance of truly understanding how any why people buy, most companies assume the already know

Most companies do NOT truly understand why customers buy

this basic information. In fact, they may become defensive if asked about their understanding of their customers. "They are OUR customers", they retort, "so certainly we know why!"

But in my experience, the sad truth is that most companies do NOT truly understand why customers buy from them or a competitor or... not at all. It's important to note that in the B2B world, fully 60% of engagements fail to result in ANY purchase behavior, according to CEB research. In other words, usually there is NO provider who meets the criteria buyers are seeking MOST of the time!

This kind of environmental work is often outdated because the marketplace is never finished evolving. At the least, new competitors are always emerging, new types of buyers or buying patterns are always evolving, the fundamental characteristics of the industry are always being reshaped by new technologies and strategic alternatives. Each of these companies let themselves fall out of step... and it nearly killed them.

2. Radical Refocus on the Customer Base

In particular, these companies focused attention on the people who were most important to their companies – the people outside their company who were their **potential customers.** They desperately needed understand with **precision and authentic detail** just why they were no longer choosing their company.

Of course, this is something that companies should always be doing. But often this "customer-centrism" becomes "nice to have" lip service. That lack of serious, bet-your-business focus on the customer is exactly what led them all – in one way or another – to get dangerously out of step with their market.

In fact, this understanding of **"why people buy"** is one of the **most valuable assets** of the company. And these companies succeeded because they not only "caught up" with the market but they gained a **competitively-superior understanding** of what drove business In their industry and that conviction helped drive their ability to deliver on it.

3. Consideration of New Options

In each of these settings, the company studied needed to explore not just the answers to the core questions in the category, but they needed to look at how the **questions changed** in their product category. That is what enabled them to look at creating dramatic new solutions.

I can't help but imagine that there was a pivotal meeting (or two!) at each of the companies in the prior chapters in which a variety of options were brainstormed and laid out for consideration. It would have been quite an experience to be a fly on those walls!

This step is the **crisis point** the transformation process. A wide range of (previously unconsidered" alternatives need to be laid out and weighed. Multiple perspectives need to be involved and considered. Finally, senior management needs to make a decision about the new direction for the product or company.

4. Commitment to a New Strategy

This step is at the **heart** the transformation process. It's here that the talk of change turns into **change** itself. For each of the companies profiled, this involved engaging everyone in the company to make significant changes to what they were doing. There are four aspects to this:

- **Clarity:** To be enacted, the corporate vision plan needs to be translated into an action plan for the company and each team member. The overall plan must be clear for each member, as does the reasons for adopting it, and why it is the best path forward.

- **Buy-in:** After understanding the plan, team members must agree to it... for the organization as well as for themselves personally. People must decide if they want to be part of the change... or not.

- **Commitment:** Beyond agreeing with the plan, the team needs to dedicate themselves to staying on plan despite opposition and obstacles. The new plan will inherently exact a higher cost than simply continuing in the same role – even if the new role is better. At the least, it involves taking on new roles working with new people in new ways, so there is an element of increased risk that people usually eschew. Accordingly, the added benefits need to be clear – including escaping from a bankrupt business model.

- **Urgency:** Everyone in the company already has a day job. This new plan gives them a different job than they originally signed up to do. This new direction needs to become THE priority, not just another one. Only one thing can be top priority. This new plan needs to push the old plan off the table or at least down the list. This is where having a real crisis can be a real advantage to infuse energy, speed, and clarity into the transition.

5. Concerted Activation of the Vision

Finally – and this is the reason each of those stories is historical and real – is that the new plan needed to get implemented. This was the true test of everything that went before. And it was the true test of the company leaders to be able to engage, motivate, and encourage all the stakeholders in the company to go beyond their original commitment to a higher level.

This is also the point at which each team member needs to evaluate for themselves personally whether they want to see themselves in the new organization. This is a deeply personal question. It also varies by each stake holder's individual situation.

I will note that the power of the brand vision can add additional energy and cohesiveness to the REpossibility effort. A company whose value is perceived as striving for something greater than itself can tap into an entirely new reservoir of human motivation.

If the company is perceived as being part of a larger movement (say, eternal love), then it is easier to get

Work on a mission work at a job

employees to see themselves as **being on a mission, not just at a job**. It was the dedication and skill in getting others on board that made the CEOs in those stories stand out so powerfully. That quality is not something that typically shows up on a resume, but that doesn't mean it can't be nurtured or encouraged.

And that brings us to the core reason for this book...

HOW YOU CAN GET THERE

The whole point of this book is to encourage you to consider and adopt new, superior business strategies that better meet the needs of your customers. Not only have companies overcome great challenges by (re)embracing their customers in the past, but we can and must do the same today. In fact, this is the kind of work I have been doing with companies for many years, whether it is focused on a product line or an entire company.

The work I do with companies usually involves one or more of the five steps above. At my firm, B2P Partners, I have developed processes for each of these issues to help companies quickly and efficiently get to the heart of the matter and start responding quickly. These can be applied to repositioning an entire company or to rejuvenating the performance of a single line of products or services.

1. Marketplace Assessment

I start with an examination of the marketing landscape your product or company faces. This helps your leadership team think about its existing challenges in new ways. The
goal is to create hypotheses (not yet answers) to the question of why you are no longer being successful. For example, we explore:

- What specifically is the **marketplace problem** we are looking to solve? When did the weakness **first appear?** Where is performance **worst?** Where is performance **best** and what might be responsible for that? Why has that strength not been translated into other markets?

- What are the **mega-trends** reshaping how people or organizations think about and address what your industry provides at the highest level? For example, Ford is re-defining its business from "automobiles" to "transportation". That may sound small or obvious, but the implications are enormous.

- Which are the **greatest external threats** to your continued success? Do they come from new kinds of buyers, new buying patterns, new technologies, or new competitors?

- How have your **buyers** and the **buying process evolved?** When is the last time you did a deep examination of how they think about the issues your industry addresses, the different ways to address that need, how they find answers, and how you and your competitors fill their bill?

Often this can be done in a few weeks for a modest sum. It is a great way to kick off an initiative with a shared experience that makes the project more tangible.

One of the most powerful ways of activating this examination is to conduct research to identify and track why your company is winning or losing deals. This "**win-loss**" analysis is very powerful for unearthing insights about:

- What **triggers** do prospects to even consider your product category?

- How do prospects start and move through the **solution consideration process**?

- What personas are involved at each stage and what role do they play?

- What is each stakeholder looking for in a **solution**?

- How is your offering **perceived** vs. alternatives by those who selected yours and those who did not?

- How does the team form a **consensus**... or not?

- This research typically takes about 4-6 weeks and costs about $20 - $30,000.

2. Key Prospect Insights

At the core of your market problem – and therefore the core of your solution – is an updated, accurate, and insightful understanding of who your customers are and why they buy (or don't in this case). Getting this understanding requires creating a set of **"buyer personas"**.

These are descriptions of proto-typical buyers as human beings (with a gender, age, job title, tenure, experience, background, etc.) so everyone in the company can identify and relate with them. More importantly, they contain a sharp description of:

- What **career goals** are prospects are looking to achieve in their jobs? Where does the issue your product addresses fit into their overall goals? We purposely start with this broad framework to put the **problem** in perspective before we start to consider how it might get solved.

- What specifically are they hoping to achieve with your offering? This is the **"job to be done"** using the framework of Clayton Christiansen.

- What **alternative strategies** do they consider? Buying your product is just one solution, but prospects will always start by considering whether the problem can be ignored or minimized by working around it, or by using other resources already on hand. Only in the case that they cannot avoid the problem or solve it on their own will they seriously consider buying your solution.

- What is their awareness and perception of **competitive offerings** vs. yours? What do they like and dislike about each? Note that this is not the typical recitation of comparative product features (which is product-centric) but rather the hierarchy of benefits your prospects seek from your offering and others (which is prospect-centric).

In the B2B (business-to-business) context, it doesn't end here because there are multiple decision makers. A persona needs to be created for each one. It is not unusual for us to discover that sales have been dropping because of the emergence of a new persona on the "buying team" or "decision-making unit".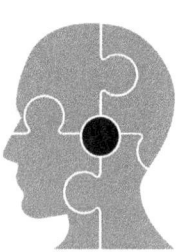

At my firm, we have been developing these personas for more than a dozen years, and have been able to hone our craft to create change-making personas for many companies. (This is outlined in greater detail in our book, Personas with Punch).

The key output of these personas is a distillation of their profile into a single, focused sentence that nails exactly how and why that persona adopts a solution. We call this the **Key Prospect Insight.** This is what gives us direction for the next step.

3. REpossibility Workshop

This is the point to bring together your decision-makers to review the intelligence you have gathered about the marketplace and your customer base in order to create **alternative go-to-market strategies.**

We are able to create new solutions because we are looking at the marketplace problems from a new perspective – what kind of offering would a person want if they could design it themselves. Our goal is to help you **create the offering your best prospects wish existed**. The workshop infuses your team with opportunistic energy and vision which helps build momentum for action.

4. Direction Selection

This is an extension of the Repossibility workshop. There are two elements to this stage.

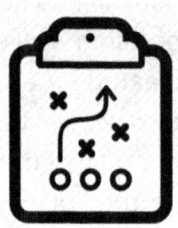

The first is getting customer and prospect input on the potential directions or offerings or positionings we have identified as most viable. We design and conduct concept tests to make this happen. This usually takes about three weeks and costs between $20 - $50,000.

The second element is a **weighted voting process** that allows for all points of view to be aired in a fair, controlled, safe environment. This also allows for thorough, meaningful conversation on the points that avoids differences of opinion becoming personality or title battles.

This can be largely completed in a day or two, depending on the complexity and size of the decision teams. The additional cost is minimal.

5. Repossibility Activation

Finally, the new plan needs to get implemented. This is the true test of everything that has gone before.

The biggest part of implementation is getting everyone on board and pulling in the same direction. This could be a book in itself.

There are consultants who are skilled at being able to make things happen. Having a dynamic, engaging CEO is a great advantage, but there are other processes that can help build momentum. Contact me if you want to learn more about these resources.

The other part of implementation is **setting benchmarks** for the results you look to change, and then taking regular measures of the progress in getting there. A robust set of metrics is crucial in keeping teams on track. Regular reporting on a weekly, monthly, and quarterly sequence is crucial for learning what is working or not and how to optimize as they went.

GETTING STARTED

Of course, a company can accomplish all these changes on its own. The companies reporting here did so themselves to a great extent. And no amount or quality of consultants can change a company. The leadership and employees MUST want to change themselves.

But I have seen situations where working with an outside catalyst can accelerate and enhance the adoption of a new strategic vision. Here are some reasons that companies look to outside resources to help them through this transition.

1. **Urgency** – a consultancy will be able to start quickly, and probably faster than internal workers who already have a "day job"

2. **Perspective** – a consultancy will have lessons learned from many different market alignment projects

3. **Experience** – a consultancy will have done this many times

4. **Independence** – unlike people already in your organization, an outside consultancy has no built-in agenda or political benefit to gain from the implementation

5. **Skills** – qualified consultants have been selected specifically to excel at this kind of process; internal people tend to need and have other skills

6. **Availability** – there is very little chance there are people in your organization with nothing else to do. It often makes sense to hire a group of people to orchestrate this change and then have them move on after the project is complete.

THIS ISN'T ALL

This is a small book of big stories. Each of these tales is the work of many unsung heroes (in addition to the celebrated ones) who invested hundreds of weekends and late nights into making those changes possible. In that sense, each one is worthy of a book in itself. Actually, there have been several books written about each of them.

But there are more.

The fact that each of these stories is remarkable doesn't mean that there are not more of them. In fact, I plan to include eight more stories in the next edition. All are stories of companies that have succeeded so much they became very large and well-known.

Many of them bring the historical perceptive of not just surviving, but thriving in the Great Depression. But the Depression wasn't the only time when these turnarounds occurred. Two of them are relatively recent turnarounds of the "Information Age".

Company	Business /Industry	Time frame
Chicago Bridge & Iron	Steel	Great Depression
Crane & Co.	Paper/ Manufacturing	Great Depression
DuPont	Chemical manufacturing	Great Depression
La-Z-Boy	Consumer durables	Great Depression
Motorola	Technology /hardware	Great Depression
RCA	Media	1930s – Advent of Television
Intel	Technology / hardware	1990s Personal Computer Boom
Cisco	Network hardware	2000s – Dot Com bust

YOUR NEXT CHAPTER

I hope this is the start of a rejuvenation in your company. I invite you to contact me at the address below to brainstorm solutions or ask advice about any of the steps.

I'd love to include your story in our next edition.

Wayne.Cerullo@B2Ppartners.com

www.B2Ppartners.com

www.ingramcontent.com/pod-product-compliance
Lightning Source LLC
Chambersburg PA
CBHW071225220526
45468CB00002B/732